It's a MoM Thing!

Kendra Smiley
illustrated by Kathy Rogers

FAITHFUL
Woman
™

Cook Communications Ministries

Faithful Woman is an imprint of
Cook Communications Ministries, Colorado Springs, Colorado 80918
Cook Communications, Paris, Ontario
Kingsway Communications, Eastbourne, England

IT'S A MOM THING
© 2000 by Kendra Smiley for text. All rights reserved.
Printed in Singapore.

1 2 3 4 5 6 7 8 9 10 Printing/Year 04 03 02 01 00

Editor: Julie Smith
Design: Oh, Wow! Brenda Franklin Creative

Library of Congress Cataloging-in-Publication Data
Smiley, Kendra
        It's a mom thing / Kendra Smiley.
            p. cm.
        ISBN 0-78143-382-7
            1. Mothers--Miscellaneous. I. Title.
    HQ759.S59 2000
    306.874'3--dc21   99-046264
                                                         CIP

To moms everywhere,
with love

He tends his flock like a shepherd:
He gathers the lambs in his arms
and carries them close to his heart;
he gently leads those that have young.

Isaiah 40:11

Contents

Introduction

Hi!

I'm a mom. Maybe you are too.

We moms are an interesting group. On one hand, we are as different as snowflakes. We come in different sizes and shapes . . . with different colors and callings . . . at different ages and abilities . . . sporting different personalities and preferences. We *all* work inside the home, and some work outside the home too. We are very different, and we are also very much alike.

Moms have been known to applaud, aggravate, correct, console, pamper, polish, scold, and snuggle their offspring—all within a matter of moments.

And most of all, moms have been known to love without reserve. We show it with our heads, our hands, and our hearts.

It's a MOM Thing!

7

It's a HEAD Thing!

She speaks with wisdom,
and faithful instruction is on her tongue.

Proverbs 31:26

It's a HEAD Thing!

Moms have a whole collection
of goofy things that they say.
Many of these sayings they learned from *their* moms.
Moms say things like, "You're grounded for life!"
When kids hear that one,
they have to wonder who is being punished.

It's a Mom Thing!

It's a HEAD Thing!

Moms say, "Have fun. Be careful."
Sometimes those two orders are mutually exclusive.
Almost all of life has some degree of risk—
especially the things that are fun—like living itself.

It's a Mom Thing!

It's a HEAD Thing!

Moms say,
"This will hurt me more than it hurts you."
(That's a line they learned from *their* moms.)
The funny thing is—it's the truth.

It's a Mom Thing!

It's a HEAD Thing!

Moms say things that used to be "in,"
but by the time they say "cool," it's really "hot."

It's a Mom Thing!

It's a HEAD Thing!

Moms say,
"Because I'm the mom, that's why,"
and kids still wonder what the answer is.
(But if they are smart, they quit asking.)

It's a Mom Thing!

It's a HEAD Thing!

Moms say,
"Think before you speak."
They also say, "Don't speak with your mouth full."
(I guess that last one applies
even if you have already been thinking.)

It's a Mom Thing!

It's a HEAD Thing!

Moms say,
"Now," which can either mean "before too long,"
or "immediately." The exact definition depends
on how many times they have already used the word.

It's a Mom Thing!

It's a HEAD Thing!

Moms say,
"Put on a sweatshirt." That means *they* are cold.

It's a Mom Thing!

It's a HAND Thing!

Whatever you do, work at it with all your heart, as working for the Lord, not for men.

Colossians 3:23

It's a HAND Thing!

Moms do lots of things because they are moms.
Moms can wash a sports uniform at breakneck speed.
In fact, they can repeat the effort tirelessly
and have their kids ready for five games in one week.

It's a Mom Thing!

It's a Hand Thing!

Moms can coordinate intricate carpooling plans.
They can actually transport multiple children to and from
activities more efficiently than most military convoys.
(Move over, General, you have nothing on today's mom.)

It's a Mom Thing!

It's a HAND Thing!

Moms can find anything!
(Maybe that's because they hid it in the first place.)

It's a Mom Thing!

TRUFF

MY HANDS

It's a HAND Thing!

Moms can transform an ordinary refrigerator door into an art gallery, proudly displaying masterpieces in crayon, watercolor, and finger paint.

It's a Mom Thing!

It's a HAND Thing!

Moms can use spit as an amazingly effective cleaning agent (until their kids get old enough to pull away).

It's a Mom Thing!

It's a HAND Thing!

What foreign matter moms cannot dissolve with spit,
they pick at with the determination
of a mother monkey.

It's a Mom Thing!

It's a HAND Thing!

Moms may go to bed,
but they do not go soundly to sleep
until everyone is safely tucked into bed.
The older their children get,
the less sleep moms require
(or is that *receive?*).

It's a Mom Thing!

It's a
ᴴₐₙᴅ Thing!

Moms can fix *almost* anything bad that happens
(especially when their kids are young).
Moms *wish* they could fix everything bad that happens.
(But that wouldn't really be a good idea.)

It's a Mom Thing!

It's a HEART Thing!

As a mother comforts her child,
so I will comfort you.

Isaiah 66:13a

It's a HEART Thing!

Moms frequently smile contentedly
and even sigh—almost imperceptibly—
at the sight of their sleeping children.

It's a Mom Thing!

It's a HEART Thing!

Moms "eat" mud pies and sand cakes
with great enjoyment.
They also spend large sums of money
at the lemonade stand,
applaud their kids' first batch of macaroni and cheese,
and savor that first cake from a mix.
It doesn't really matter how anything tastes.

It's a Mom Thing!

It's a HEART Thing!

Moms have incredibly soft laps.
So do grandmas.
It's almost a shame when the kids
get too big to enjoy them.

It's a Mom Thing!

It's a
HEART Thing!

Moms are cheerleaders.
They cheer when their children succeed.
They cheer up their children when they don't succeed.
And perhaps more importantly,
they cheer their children
as their children cheer those who succeed
and cheer up those who don't succeed.

It's a Mom Thing!

It's a HEART Thing!

Moms are "hear-leaders."
They listen to their children.
They listen to the Word of God,
and they help their children
listen to the Word of God too.

It's a Mom Thing!

It's a HEART Thing!

Moms are "tear-leaders."
They are compassionate and really do care
that the day was crummy.

It's a Mom Thing!

It's a HEART Thing!

Moms almost always try to give
their kids the benefit of the doubt.
But if moms doubt that extending the benefit
is in their children's best interest,
they will rule accordingly.

It's a Mom Thing!

It's a HEART Thing!

Moms may or may not have been in attendance
at their children's conception.
It is a good plan, but it is not necessary.

It's a Mom Thing!

May our Lord Jesus Christ himself

and God our Father, who loved us

and by his grace gave us eternal encouragement

and good hope, encourage your hearts

and strengthen you in every good deed

and word .

2 Thessalonians 2:16

So Do YOUR Thing, MOM!

As you can see, we moms are each complex and unique beings, yet we do have some things in common. All of us are on an exciting adventure, one that began the day we became mothers and never really ends.

The adventure? Motherhood. It can provide a challenge and a chuckle. Often delightful and occasionally disastrous . . . both exhausting and enlightening . . . equally perilous and positive. It is the most difficult job any woman can tackle, and yet with benefits beyond compare.

So as you navigate this adventure, take heart. You are not alone. Laugh, love, and learn. And most of all, enjoy TODAY, for this is not a dress rehearsal. And finding enjoyment in each and every day is, after all, a MOM thing!

Love and joy to you
from Matthew, Aaron, and Jonathan's Mom,

Kendra